Men, Women and Children

in

The Second World War

Peter Hepplewhite

WAYLAND

First published in 2010 by Wayland

Copyright © Wayland 2010

Wayland
338 Euston Road
London NW1 3BH

Wayland
Level 17/207 Kent Stree[t]
Sydney, NSW 2000

British Library Cataloguing in Publication Data
Hepplewhite, Peter
   Men, women and children in the Second World War
   1. World War, 1939-1945 - Social aspects - Juvenile literature
   2. World War, 1939-1945 - Social aspects - Great Britain - Juvenile literature
   3. Great Britain - History - George VI, 1936-1952 - Juvenile literature
   I. Title
   940.5'31-dc22

ISBN: 978 0 7502 6237 8

Printed in China

Wayland is a division of Hachette Children's Books, an Hachette UK Company.
www.hachette.co.uk

Picture acknowledgments: Eggit/Fox Photos/Getty Images: Cover (main), 9; Evening Standard/Getty Images: 20; Fox Photos/Hulton Archive/Getty Images: Cover (BL), 19; Eric Harlow/Keystone/Getty Images: Cover (CL), 13; Peter Hepplewhite: 4, 18T, 22, 23, 24, 28; Hulton Archive/Getty Images: 12, 26; Keystone/Getty Images: 17; Keystone Features/Getty Images: 16; Popperfoto/Getty Images: 18B; Punch Ltd/TopFoto.co.uk: 15; Selznik/MGM/Courtesy Kobal Collection: 25; Shutterstock: Backgrounds; Reg Speller/Getty Images: 27; Ian Thompson: 6; ©TopFoto/TopFoto.co.uk: 21; William Vanderson/Hulton Archive: 5, 11; Photo by William Vandivert/Time & Life Pictures/Getty Images: 14; Wayland Archive: Cover (TL), 3, 7, 8, 10

Contents

Words that appear in **bold**
can be found in the glossary
on page 28.

WHY DID BRITAIN GO TO WAR?

When Britain declared war on Germany on 3rd September 1939, a joke soon spread across the country: **'Ding! Ding! Round 2'**. Children who knew their history got it straightaway. Everyone over 40 had lived through World War One, the terrible conflict that led to the defeat of Germany in 1918. The joke meant that the new war was like scene from a boxing match. The enemy had not been knocked out in round one and the fight was on again.

GERMANY THREATENS

In 1933 Adolf Hitler and the **Nazi Party** came to power In Germany. Hitler promised to be a strong leader and make his nation great again. In March 1938 Nazi troops took over Austria. Six months later Hitler claimed the Sudetenland, part of Czechoslovakia, for Germany.

Britain's prime minister, Neville Chamberlain, met Hitler for crisis talks. Reluctantly Chamberlain agreed to his claims – on condition that Hitler asked for nothing more. This uneasy peace lasted until March 1939 when the German army occupied the rest of Czechoslovakia. When Hitler attacked Poland on the 1st September 1939 Britain was at last forced to act.

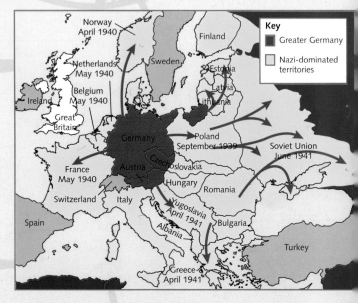

▲ This map shows the extent to which the Nazis were dominant in Europe by June 1941.

THE WORLD WAR TWO TIMELINE

1941 Conscription of women for war work begins.

1944 D-Day landings in Normandy. V1 rocket attacks on southern England.

| 1939 | 1940 | 1941 | 1942 | 1943 | 1944 | 1945 | 1946 |

1st September: Germany invades Poland. Evacuation begins. 3rd September: War declared.

January: rationing begins. Summer: Dunkirk evacuation; Home Guard called up; Battle of Britain.

7th September: Blitz begins

1943 War work made compulsory for all women aged 18-50. 20th January: Sandhurst Road School, London, bombed.

8th May: Victory in Europe Day.

PREPARING FOR WAR

The British had already been preparing for war for months. 200,000 young men had been called up for **military** training – the first of millions who would join the armed services. 1,400,000 men and women had become **Air Raid Precautions** (ARP) volunteers to protect **civilians** during attacks by enemy aircraft – or invasion.

▲ Council workers hand out kits for Anderson shelters, ready to be bolted together in back gardens.

Over two million air raid shelters were issued to families with gardens and almost 40 million gas masks handed out in case German bombers dropped gas or chemical bombs. Schools, factories and offices had regular drills with people rushing to cellars or newly dug air raid trenches while pulling on their gas masks. Getting on with work and family life in these trying times was called the 'Home Front'.

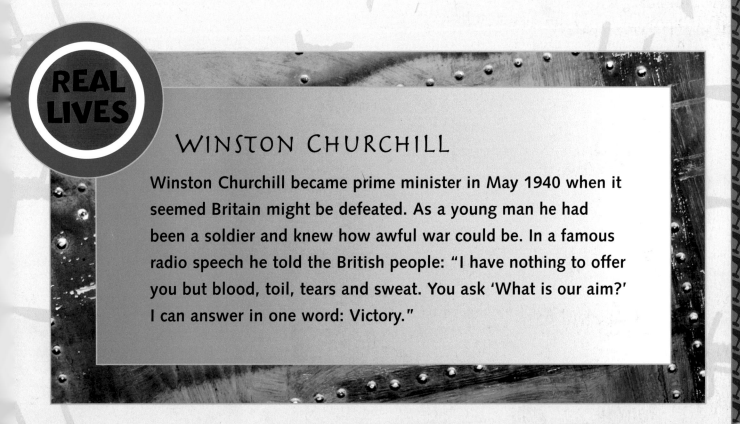

REAL LIVES

WINSTON CHURCHILL

Winston Churchill became prime minister in May 1940 when it seemed Britain might be defeated. As a young man he had been a soldier and knew how awful war could be. In a famous radio speech he told the British people: "I have nothing to offer you but blood, toil, tears and sweat. You ask 'What is our aim?' I can answer in one word: Victory."

WHY WERE CHILDREN EVACUATED?

During the First World War, 1,400 people in Britain had been killed in air raids. Since then aircraft had become bigger and faster and the British government feared that many cities would be devastated by German bombers. As many as 600,000 civilian dead and twice as many injured were expected in the first 60 days of war.

SAVE THE CHILDREN

In 1938, with this grim picture in mind, plans were made to save as many mothers, children and disabled people as possible by moving them to safety. This was called the Evacuation Scheme. Towns and cities at risk from air raids were designated 'evacuation zones'.

When the war began millions of people would be moved into country areas known as 'reception zones'. No one was forced to go but parents were told that it was their duty to send their children to safety.

▼ Evacuees queue to board a train. Older children were expected to look out for the younger boys and girls.

▲ Most evacuees wore labels in case they got lost. Information on the labels included their name, home address, school and destination.

ON THE MOVE

When Germany invaded Poland on 1st September 1939, the biggest movement of people in British history began. Over the next few days hundreds of thousands of school children, teachers and helpers, and mothers with young children, as well as 13,000 pregnant women and 7,000 blind and disabled people took part in the official evacuation. They were all moved without a single serious accident.

When the evacuees arrived in the reception areas, **billeting officers** found them homes with local families.

REAL LIVES

AGNES CONWAY, EVACUEE

In 2002, when she was 74, Agnes Conway recalled her experiences as an 11-year-old evacuee from Newcastle:
"I left with my school on Friday 1st September 1939. I carried a small case with a change of underwear and my pyjamas. I thought we were only going for two weeks. We travelled by train in compartments of eight seats. We were a mixture of ages so the older girls could look after the young ones. I stayed in Kendal with Mr and Mrs King. Looking back I think they were quite poor and needed the **billeting money**."

WHAT HAPPENED TO EVACUEES?

Many evacuees thoroughly enjoyed themselves. They had welcoming foster families and found country life an adventure. Soon 'the **townies**' were helping out with pheasant shoots, snaring rabbits, milking cows or bringing in the harvest. Even when schools reopened the lessons were often randomly put together. Evacuees were taught in church halls with almost no equipment. In fine weather lessons were nature rambles or farm visits, in bad weather classes put on plays, concerts and debates.

◀ These evacuees are enjoying outdoor lessons on a farm. Many evacuees shared schools with local children.

EVACUATION FAILURE

However, although the government didn't admit it during the war, the Evacuation Scheme was a failure. By Christmas 1939 around two out of every three evacuees had returned home. Cities had not been attacked and parents wanted their children back with them.

A lot of evacuees had an unhappy time and were mistreated. Some hosts didn't like having to look after 'other people's kids', while a number were too old or busy to care for children properly. Evacuee Doreen Manwaring remembered: 'We had so little to eat we were reduced to eating anything, lumps of dried bread and cake crumbs.'

EVACUATION SCANDAL

Evacuation also caused uncovered a national scandal – poverty. Many evacuees came from poor homes blighted by unemployment. Their dreadful condition shocked their new hosts. Children from inner city slums arrived dirty and lice infested, with no change of clothes. Some did not know how to use a toilet, had rarely eaten a hot meal and never seen a green vegetable. After a storm of complaints the government hurriedly ordered the medical inspection of evacuees.

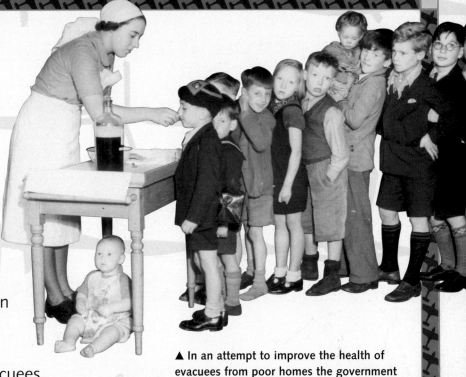

▲ In an attempt to improve the health of evacuees from poor homes the government gave free school milk and cod liver oil to all children under five.

REAL LIVES

MICHAEL CAINE, EVACUEE

Famous actor Michael Caine has written about his miserable evacuation with a foster mother in Berkshire:
"I was just six years old. She used to go away for the weekend and lock us up in a dark cupboard under the stairs. She would only let us out in time to go to school on Monday morning. **Malnutrition** gave me sores on my legs. We only ate tinned pilchards. But what always worried me was that the teachers never noticed anything strange. I suppose during the war they had other things on their mind."

How were people protected from air raids?

During the war, 60,000 people died in air raids and 85,000 were seriously injured. This total was far fewer than expected but still dreadful. The first large air raid on London came at 4.56 pm on 7th September 1940 – the start of the **Blitz**.

▲ This double-decker bus in Balham, London, fell into an enormous bomb crater during the Blitz in October 1940.

The Blitz begins

The German Air Force sent 350 fighters and bombers to attack the docks in the East End of London. As darkness fell, both sides of the river were ablaze. Grain stores burst into flames, hot sugar melted and burned on the water, rum barrels exploded. The raiders came again every night for the next 57 nights.

Other towns were soon hit too. When Coventry was bombed on November 14th 1940, 554 people were killed. On 13th -14th March 1941, 528 people died in the shipbuilding town of Clydebank.

Anti-aircraft defences

British air defences hit back at German air raids. **RADAR** detected enemy bombers over the sea, giving time for night-fighters to catch them. As they crossed the coast 'Ack-Acks' (anti-aircraft guns) opened fire on the enemy planes. Finally, huge **barrage balloons** hung like tethered silver whales over target areas, ready to rip the wings off low flying bombers.

ARP

When the bombers got through, Air Raid Precautions took over. Every street or local area had a warden who guided people to shelters when the air raid sirens wailed. When bombs fell, the wardens telephoned reports to local control rooms. ARP Control staff then sent the fire, ambulance, rescue or first aid squads to the most urgent incidents.

A quarter of all ARP staff were women, including fire watchers, wardens and ambulance drivers.

▼ An ARP warden helps a mother and her children practise wearing their gas masks.

REAL LIVES

LEMONADE FACTORY DISASTER

At 11.12 pm on Saturday May 3rd 1941 the air raid sirens sounded over North Shields. Nearly 200 people hurried to the large shelter under Wilkinson's lemonade factory. At midnight, a single bomb from a lone German raider scored a direct hit on the three storey building. Walls and machinery collapsed into the shelter. 107 people, 41 of them children, were killed. The first reports of the disaster were recorded by ARP wardens involved in the rescue of the survivors.

HOW DID PEOPLE PREPARE FOR INVASION?

Britain came close to defeat in the summer of 1940. In April, Denmark and Norway fell to Nazi troops while in May the German **Blitzkrieg** – or lightning war – smashed through Belgium and Holland into France. The British army, fighting alongside the French, was cut off and fell back to the port of Dunkirk. Defeat and surrender seemed only a matter of time.

THE MIRACLE OF DUNKIRK

▲ This dramatic painting by Charles Cundall, a war artist for the Royal Navy, shows the Navy rescuing the British army from the beaches of Dunkirk.

On 29th May the Royal Navy began a desperate rescue bid, 'Operation Dynamo'. Against all the odds, German troops stopped their advance and the weather stayed calm. Over the next week the Navy pulled out almost 340,000 troops from Dunkirk and nearby beaches. The Navy was helped by 700 'little ships': fishing boats, channel ferries and private yachts, all crewed by civilians.

THE HOME GUARD

To help in the emergency the government called for recruits to join a new defence force – the Home Guard. By the end of July over a million men aged between 17 and 65 had been given makeshift training to fight German paratroops and **saboteurs** and protect important factories.

THE BATTLE OF BRITAIN

On 16th July Hitler ordered his generals to draw up plans for Operation Sea Lion, the invasion of Britain. First the *Luftwaffe*, the German Air Force, had to take control of the skies – but the British RAF was able and waiting.

Top secret RADAR stations detected German planes soon after they took off and fed the information to control rooms. Hurricane and Spitfire fighters were sent up day after day to intercept the German attacks. After two

▲ The Royal Air Force battles a Nazi winged devil in this cartoon which was published in *Punch* magazine.

months of bitter fighting the *Luftwaffe* was beaten and Sea Lion was cancelled. Britain was saved.

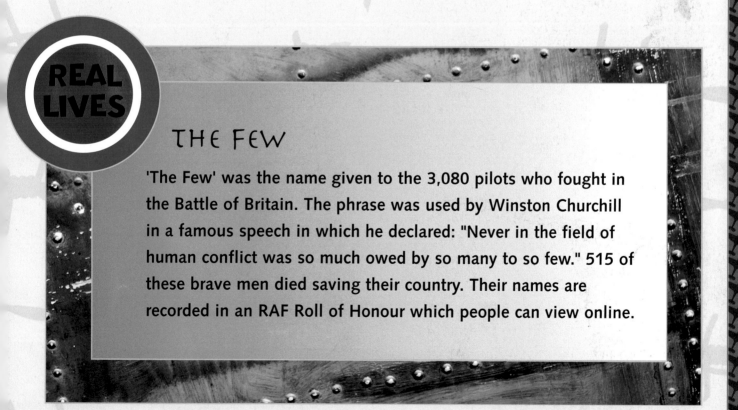

REAL LIVES

THE FEW

'The Few' was the name given to the 3,080 pilots who fought in the Battle of Britain. The phrase was used by Winston Churchill in a famous speech in which he declared: "Never in the field of human conflict was so much owed by so many to so few." 515 of these brave men died saving their country. Their names are recorded in an RAF Roll of Honour which people can view online.

WHAT JOBS DID MEN DO DURING THE WAR?

The working lives of most adults changed dramatically with the outbreak of war. Most fit young men had to fight. In April 1939 the government began to **conscript** or 'call up' those aged 18-22, but this was soon changed to include all men between the ages of 18 and 41. At first, they were allowed to choose between the army, the navy and the air force, but later in the war were told which service to join.

▲ Members of the Royal Marines wait to disembark from a landing craft. They were taking part in an invasion exercise in December 1942.

THE ARMED FORCES

To wage war all over the world the armed forces had to grow hugely. By 1945 2,920,000 men were soldiers, with another 900,000 in the Royal Navy and a million in the RAF. Recruits had to leave their families and spend months in training camps. Once they were posted abroad it could be years before they came home on leave.

INDUSTRY AT WAR

To win the war Britain needed to produce vast quantities of weapons and ammunition but with so many men in the armed services there was a shortage of workers. Ernest Bevin, the Minister of Labour, was given powers to order people to do any job anywhere in the country. Some men, including dock and railway

◀ Bevin boys prepare to go underground to start their training at Markham Main Colliery, near Doncaster, in September 1943.

workers, had jobs that were so important they were not allowed to leave them. Others, such as the 21,000 '**Bevin Boys**', were sent to work in the coal mines.

Older factory workers had to adapt quickly to wartime work. In June 1940, when the British army had only 100 tanks left, Vauxhall Motors in Luton was ordered to build Churchill tanks. The Raleigh bicycle factory in Nottingham switched to making 20mm cartridges, the bullets fired by Spitfires and Hurricanes.

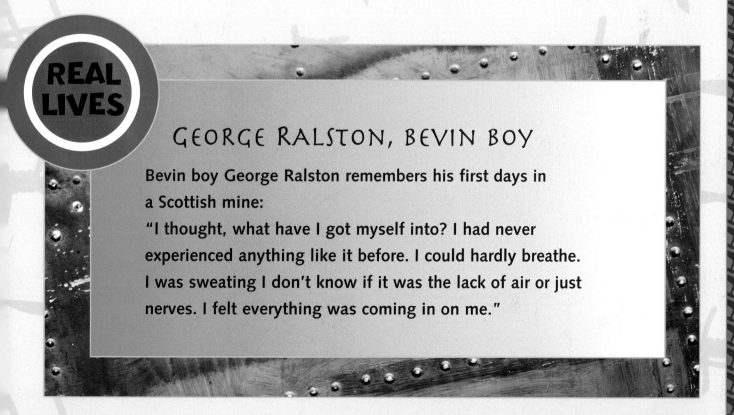

REAL LIVES

GEORGE RALSTON, BEVIN BOY

Bevin boy George Ralston remembers his first days in a Scottish mine:

"I thought, what have I got myself into? I had never experienced anything like it before. I could hardly breathe. I was sweating I don't know if it was the lack of air or just nerves. I felt everything was coming in on me."

WHAT JOBS DID WOMEN DO DURING THE WAR?

By 1941 there were millions of jobs to be filled, everywhere from the factories to the farms. To meet this crisis, the government began to conscript women for the first time in British history. By mid-1943, almost 90 per cent of single women and 80 per cent of married women were employed in essential work for the war effort – whether they liked it or not! By 1945, 7.5 million women had been called up.

▶ Government campaigns such as this one encouraged women to help the war effort.

How will **our girls respond?**

Driver or Mechanic

A180562

Kine-Theodolite Operator

● **All this is vital work** and there are many other important jobs.

Catering

Orderly

500 South Shields Girls are asked to **Volunteer for the ATS**

Go now and have a talk at your local Employment Exchange or A.T.S. or Army Recruiting Centre.

You can enrol at the Employment Exchange in Wawn Street, South Shields. Why not call there now?

INTO THE ARMED SERVICES

Over 450,000 women joined the armed service; they did not have to fight but some came close to it. The women's branch of the army was called the Auxiliary Territorial Service (ATS). ATS squads operated searchlights and anti-aircraft guns during air raids.

Women who wanted to join the RAF signed up for the Women's Auxiliary Air Force. WAAF pilots delivered aircraft, including fighters, to front line squadrons.

▶ This woman is inspecting a Merlin engine at the Rolls Royce factory near Glasgow in 1942. Merlin engines were used to power many British aircraft during the Second World War.

WOMEN IN INDUSTRY

Most women went into essential industries, working as **lathe** operators in aircraft factories, welders in shipyards and operating signals on the railways. Hours were long and working conditions often hard and dirty. Fancy clothing was a thing of the past as they swapped skirts for trousers or dungarees and headscarves to stop their hair being trapped in machinery.

WOMEN ON FARMS

German U-boats (submarines) came close to cutting off supplies to Britain in 1940-41. To beat this threat, 80,000 women joined the Women's Land Army, helping to grow food. 'Land Girls' lived in local hostels or on farms, doing everything from milking cows and mucking out the cow shed to planting potatoes and repairing potato sacks.

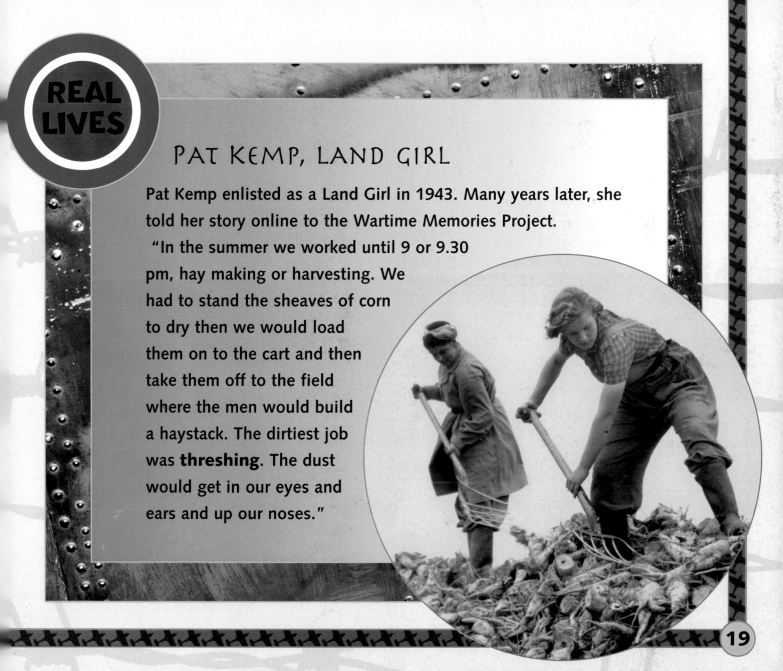

REAL LIVES

PAT KEMP, LAND GIRL

Pat Kemp enlisted as a Land Girl in 1943. Many years later, she told her story online to the Wartime Memories Project.

"In the summer we worked until 9 or 9.30 pm, hay making or harvesting. We had to stand the sheaves of corn to dry then we would load them on to the cart and then take them off to the field where the men would build a haystack. The dirtiest job was **threshing**. The dust would get in our eyes and ears and up our noses."

WHAT WAS SCHOOL LIKE DURING THE WAR?

To the delight of many children, World War II began with the government ordering the mass closure of schools. Although only one in three young people were evacuated, more than half the teachers went with them. With a shortage of staff local schools remained shut for months.

◀ These eager children are donating scrap metal to help build weapons. Unfortunately much of the scrap that people collected was of poor quality and so was never used.

CHAOS AND CHANGE

By October 1939 there were complaints all over the country that children in the cities were running wild. To the relief of desperate parents, thousands of makeshift classrooms were set up in homes or church halls. Lessons included lots of field work with trips to museums and parks. Most schools were reopened by the summer of 1940, but they were quite different. Young male teachers had joined up and been replaced by married women. Before the war female teachers had to give up their jobs if they married.

AIR RAID PRACTICE

Many schools remained closed until they were equipped with air raid shelters. Children practised hurrying to the shelters while putting their gas masks on. If there was an air raid late at night, classes had a half day off to catch up with their sleep.

DISASTER

School disasters shook the country too. On 20th January 1943, Sandhurst Road School in Catford, London, took a direct hit from a 250 kg bomb. The school burst into flames and 38 children between the ages of 5 and 15 died, together with six teachers. 150 more children were seriously injured.

▶ Rescue workers search for survivors and bodies in the wreckage of Sandhurst Road School. The school was bombed in a daylight raid in January 1943.

REAL LIVES

ERIC BRADY, SCHOOLBOY CASUALTY

Eric Brady was disabled in the bombing of Sandhurst Road School. His older sister Kitty was killed. In 2008 he recalled: "More children than usual were running around the playground that day because we were going to a performance of 'A Midsummer Night's Dream' that afternoon, and the bomber pilot must have seen them." Eric was eating his sandwiches in the school's ground floor dining area when the bomb hit directly over it. It was hours before he was dug out of the rubble.

HOW DID PEOPLE 'MAKE DO' DURING THE WAR?

One battle was fought every day throughout World War II – the Battle of the Atlantic. The Royal Navy escorted convoys of merchant ships carrying vital supplies from North America to Britain. On the long crossing they were under constant threat from 'wolf packs' of German U-boats. Thousands of their vessels were torpedoed and sunk.

Your own vegetables all the year round . . . if you DIG FOR VICTORY NOW

▲ Almost 1,500,000 families had allotments during the war. Food that people grew for themselves was not rationed.

DIG FOR VICTORY

The 'Dig for Victory' **campaign** encouraged people to grow their own fruit and vegetables and to keep hens or rabbits in their gardens. Children sometimes got upset when the time came to slaughter these animals for meat. Parks and school playing fields were turned into allotments. Hyde Park in London even had its own piggery.

RATIONING

Soon goods of all kinds were scarce and in January 1940 the Ministry of Food introduced rationing to share provisions fairly. Everyone was issued with a ration book containing coupons that were torn out by the shopkeeper when goods were bought. By 1943 weekly rations per person included: butter 2½ oz (72g), cheese 1 oz (28g), sweets 2 oz (72g) and tea 2 oz (56g).

I'm an Energy Food!

Says **'POTATO PETE'**

HEALTHY EATING

'Dr Carrot' and 'Potato Pete' were cartoon characters used in adverts to encourage families to eat healthy foods. Young children, pregnant women and nursing mothers were given extra rations of cod-liver oil, orange juice and milk. Surprisingly the health of wartime children improved. On average they were taller and heavier than children today!

MAKE DO AND MEND

Most essential items such as petrol and clothes were also rationed. Unable to buy stockings, many women rubbed gravy onto their legs instead. Knitting became a particularly useful pastime. Campaigns such as 'Make do and Mend' and 'Sew and Save' gave advice on recycling or making clothing last longer.

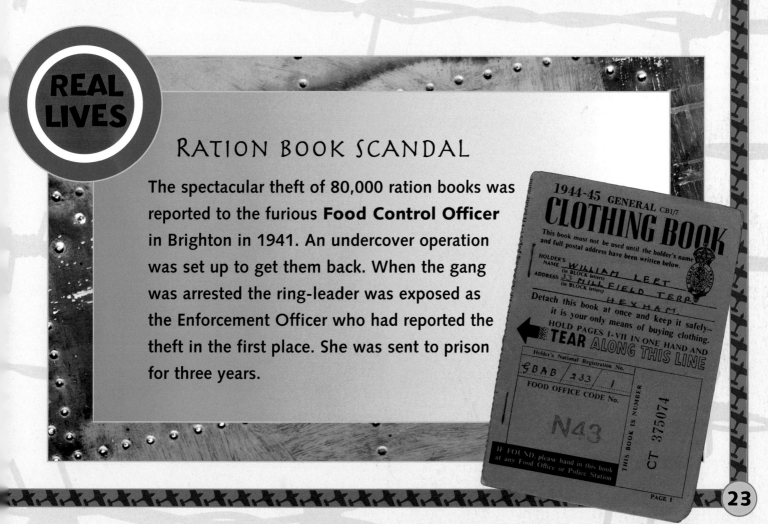

REAL LIVES

RATION BOOK SCANDAL

The spectacular theft of 80,000 ration books was reported to the furious **Food Control Officer** in Brighton in 1941. An undercover operation was set up to get them back. When the gang was arrested the ring-leader was exposed as the Enforcement Officer who had reported the theft in the first place. She was sent to prison for three years.

HOW DID PEOPLE HAVE FUN DURING THE WAR?

Places of entertainment such as cinemas, theatres and sports grounds were closed when the war began – in case they were hit in an air raid and people were killed. Most were reopened within weeks however, when the government realised that having fun was important for **morale**.

DANCING AND SPORT

Every town and village had a hall where dancing could take place. The bigger dance halls had orchestras, the smaller ones had a three piece band or played records. With the arrival of American soldiers the 'jitterbug' became a dance craze. But wild moves, such as sliding your partner between your legs, shocked older dancers, and jitterbugging was banned from many halls.

Football had its problems too. Not only had most of the top players joined up, but the government imposed a 50-mile travelling limit to matches to save petrol. At times grounds were closed for other, grimmer uses; in 1940 the East Stand at White Hart Lane (Tottenham Hotspur's home ground) was used as a mortuary for victims of the Blitz.

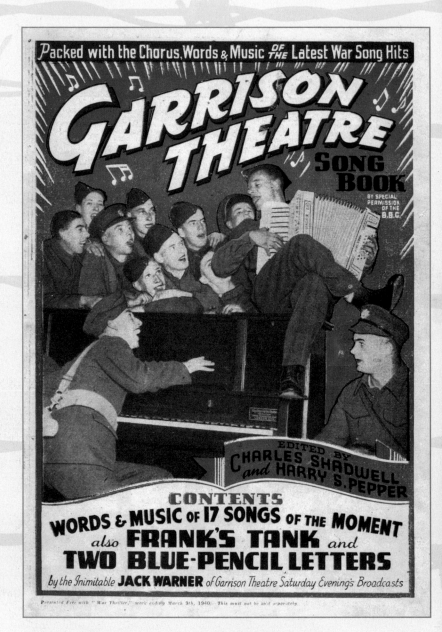

▲ Garrison Theatre was a popular radio programme. Using song sheets like this, listeners could sing along with the stars.

CINEMA AND HOLIDAYS

Many people went to the cinema two or three times a week, so a night out at the 'pictures' usually began with a wait in a long queue. Patriotic films such as *In Which We Serve* or *Target for Tonight* showed the bravery of the armed forces, but the most popular films all came from Hollywood.

With beaches off limits for the war, and to cut unnecessary journeys, the government encouraged people to take 'Holidays at Home'. Local councils organised special programmes of events including fun fairs, concerts, pageants and special teas.

DAVID O. SELZNICK'S PRODUCTION OF MARGARET MITCHELL'S

"GONE WITH THE WIND"

STARRING

CLARK GABLE
VIVIEN LEIGH
LESLIE HOWARD
OLIVIA de HAVILLAND

Winner of Ten Academy Awards

▶ Love stories such as *Gone with the Wind* helped wartime cinema-goers forget about the bombs for an evening.

REAL LIVES

ITMA AND TOMMY HANDLEY

Listening to the radio was a favourite way to relax during the war. Every week around 16 million people tuned in to the top comedy programme, ITMA. The name was a joke about Hitler. In the 1930s, whenever Hitler made a new territorial claim the newspaper headlines would proclaim 'It's That Man Again'. Tommy Handley starred as the Minister of Aggravation in the Office of Twerps and made fun of the endless wartime rules that irritated the British people.

WHAT HAPPENED TO PEOPLE WHEN THE WAR ENDED?

After seven years of hard fighting, the Second World War ended in 1945. Britain celebrated Victory in Europe (VE) Day on the 8th May and Victory in Japan (VJ Day) on 15th August. The cost of the war was high, with 338,000 military staff and civilians dead and over a million injured.

FAMILIES BACK TOGETHER

Many children saw their fathers for the first time in years. Thirty thousand servicemen a week were '**demobbed**' – more than a million by December 1945. Each man was given a suit, two shirts, a raincoat and a trilby hat. Around 200,000 British prisoners of war came home too, many in a terrible condition from maltreatment in enemy prison camps.

Some men found it hard to cope, missing the companionship and excitement of service life or suffering what we now call **post traumatic stress disorder.**

AUSTERITY BRITAIN

The years after the war were known as a time of austerity – hardship and shortages. Britain had almost gone bankrupt paying for the war and needed a huge loan from the USA. Rationing not only continued but for a while became stricter. The meat allowance was at its smallest in 1951 and sweet rationing lasted until 1953.

▶ A US soldier greets his English wife and their baby son on their arrival in New York from London in 1945. The couple had met when the soldier was stationed in England during the war.

CHANGING TIMES

To widespread surprise Winston Churchill lost the general election in 1945 and a Labour government took power. Labour introduced a series of reforms that became known as the welfare state. The most important part of this was the National Health Service, set up in 1948. The NHS offered free health care to all. There was a huge backlog of patients. The £2 million put aside to pay for free spectacles over the first nine months of the NHS was spent in six weeks.

▲ Children sit at V-shaped tables at a street party in south London. Parties like this were held all over Britain to celebrate VE Day (Victory in Europe) in May 1945.

REAL LIVES

A COUPLE REUNITED

In 1945 Miss Littleboy met her boyfriend for the first time in three years. He was a survivor of a Japanese prisoner of war camp. In her diary she described her shock at seeing how much the war had made him suffer:

"This was not the young man I had known. Misshapen, pitted, scarred. Only the eyes were the same. I looked at this hulk of humanity and my heart bled. Could I keep this man alive and help him get back into life again?"

GLOSSARY

Air Raid Precautions (ARP): The organisation and personnel that protected and rescued people during air raids.

barrage balloons: Massive balloons tied to the ground, used to damage low-flying enemy planes.

Bevin Boys: Young men who were sent to work in the coal mines instead of the armed forces.

billeting money: Payment made to people in return for providing accommodation for evacuees.

billeting officers: Officials who were in charge of finding accommodation for evacuees with host families.

Blitz: Intensive bombing of British cities by the German Air Force during 1940-1941.

Blitzkrieg: German for 'lightning war': fast-moving armies and air attacks.

campaign: Government publicity campaign.

civilian: A member of the public who is not in the military or the police service.

conscript: Compel a person to join the armed forces.

demobbed: Short for demobilized, meaning released from military service.

Food Control Officer: Local official in charge of enforcing rationing.

lathe: A precision machine for making parts for other machines, like aircraft.

malnutrition: Badly fed, even half starved.

military: Members of the armed services, the army, navy and airforce.

morale: The way people feel about a war and if they believe their side can win.

Nazi Party: The German National Socialist Party, led by Adolf Hitler.

post traumatic stress disorder: Depression, shock or flashbacks caused by the terrible things troops had seen on the battlefields.

RADAR: Short for Radio Detection and Ranging. A way of detecting aircraft by bouncing radio waves off them.

saboteurs: Enemy spies and small attack squads hitting targets such as bridges or railways.

threshing: Beating cereal plants to separate the seeds from the straw.

townies: Nickname for evacuees because most of them came from towns and cities.

FURTHER INFORMATION

MORE BOOKS TO READ

Simon Adams
In the War: The Blitz and
Evacuation
(Wayland, 2010)

Alan Childs
**The Daily Life of: A World
War II Evacuee**
(Wayland, 2008)

Alison Cooper
**The War Years: The Home
Front**
(Wayland, 2007)

Liz Gogerly
**The Home Front:
Reconstructed**
(Wayland, 2005)

Peter Hepplewhite
An Evacuee's Journey
(Wayland, 2004)

Peter Hicks
In the War: Food and Rations
and **School Life**
(Wayland, 2010)

USEFUL WEBSITES

http://www.cwgc.org/
Search the Dept of Honour Register for the
names of the 1.7 million war dead from both
World War I and II. The names of people who
were killed in air raids are included.

www.westallswar.org
A detailed look at the bombing incident that
destroyed the public air raid shelter in
Wilkinson's Lemonade Factory in North Shields.

**http://www.bbc.co.uk/history/worldwars/wwt
wo/**
BBC history site on the Second World War.

**http://www.bbc.co.uk/schools/primaryhistory
/world_war2/**
Explore what it was like to be a child during
the Second World War at this BBC website.

**http://www.nms.ac.uk/our_museums/war_mu
seum.aspx**
The National War Museum, Scotland tells the
story of Scotland at war through the ages.

PLACES TO VISIT

Eden Camp, Malton, North Yorkshire
A prisoner of war camp turned into a stunning
World War II theme park.
http://www.edencamp.co.uk/

Imperial War Museum, London
The best war museum in the country.
http://london.iwm.org.uk/

Newhaven Fort, Newhaven
Experience an air raid and visit the
gun emplacements.
http://www.newhavenfort.org.uk/

Imperial War Museum, Duxford
An awesome collection of war planes. Don't
forget to visit the Land Warfare Hall, too.
http://duxford.iwm.org.uk/

Winston Churchill's Britain at War Experience
London Bridge, London
Experience the fury of the Blitz from inside
an air raid shelter.
http://www.britainatwar.co.uk/

Index

Numbers in **bold** indicate pictures.